Written for the London Sinfonietta for Oliver Knussen's 50th Birthday

First performed on 12 June 2000 by members of the London Sinfonietta
(John Orford, bassoon, and Paul Silverthorne, viola)
at Queen Elizabeth Hall, London

First recorded by Peter Kolkay, bassoon and Maureen Gallagher, viola,
on Bridge Records 9128

Duration: 3 minutes

T0081464

NOTE BY THE COMPOSER

The title of this piece was suggested by Arnold Schoenberg's short story "To the Wharfs" in which he describes the mounting anxiety of the members of a French fishing village as the boats and the sea-bound fisherman failed to appear after a storm and several days' absence. When they were suddenly sighted all shouted "to the wharfs, *aux quais*, O.K."

—Elliott Carter

ANMERKUNG DES KOMPONISTEN

Der Titel dieses Stückes wurde von Arnold Schoenbergs Kurzgeschichte "To the Wharfs" ("Zu den Kais") inspiriert, worin die immer größer werdende Besorgnis der Einwohner eines französischen Fischerdorfes beschrieben wird, als die Boote der seefahrenden Fischer nach einem Sturm und einigen Tagen der Abwesenheit nicht zurückkommen. Als sie unerwartet doch erscheinen, wird überall gerufen "zu den Kais, aux quais, OK!"

—Elliott Carter

NOTE DU COMPOSITEUR

Le titre de ce morceau a été inspiré par la nouvelle d'Arnold Schoenberg « To the Wharfs » (Aux quais) où il décrit l'inquiétude grandissante des habitants d'un village de pêche français qui, après une tempête, ne voient pas revenir les pêcheurs et leurs bateaux pendant plusieurs jours. Quand soudainement ils apparaissent tout le monde crie : « Aux quais, O.K. ».

—Elliott Carter

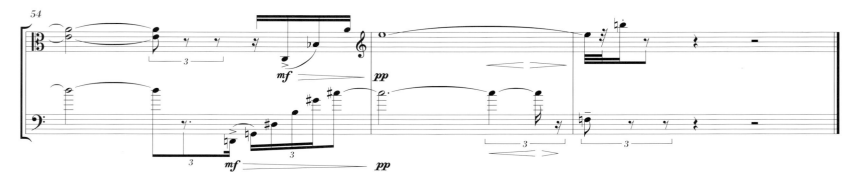

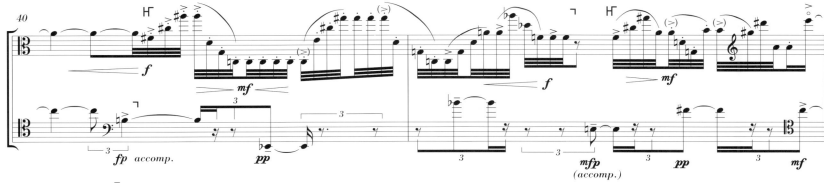

CHAMBER MUSIC OF
ELLIOTT CARTER

TRIPLE DUO (1983)   20'
for flute (doubling piccolo), clarinet (doubling E♭ and
bass clarinets), percussion, piano, violin, and cello

CHANGES (1983)   7'
for guitar

CANON FOR 4 (1984)   4'
"Homage to William"
for flute, bass clarinet, violin and cello

RICONOSCENZA PER GOFFREDO
   PETRASSI (1984)   4'
for solo violin

ESPRIT RUDE / ESPRIT DOUX (1984)   4'
pour Pierre Boulez
for flute and B♭ clarinet

STRING QUARTET NO. 4 (1986)   24'

ENCHANTED PRELUDES (1988)   6'
for flute and cello

BIRTHDAY FLOURISH (1988)   1'
for five trumpets or brass quintet

CON LEGGEREZZA PENSOSA (1990)   5'
Omaggio a Italo Calvino
for B♭ clarinet, violin, and cello

SCRIVO IN VENTO (1991)   5'
for solo flute

QUINTET (1991)   20'
for piano and winds

TRILOGY (1992)   17'
   Bariolage *for solo harp*   7'
   Inner Song *for solo oboe*   5'
   Immer Neu *for oboe and harp*   5'

GRA (1993)   4'
for solo B♭ clarinet

GRA (1993)   4'
transcribed for trombone by Benny Sluchin

TWO FIGMENTS
for solo cello
   No. 1 (1994)   5'
   No. 2 – Remembering Mr. Ives (2001)   3'

TWO FRAGMENTS
for string quartet
   No. 1 – in memoriam David Huntley (1994)   4'
   No. 2 (1999)   3'

ESPRIT RUDE / ESPRIT DOUX II (1994)   5'
for flute, clarinet and marimba

OF CHALLENGE AND OF LOVE (1995)   25'
five poems of John Hollander
for soprano and piano

STRING QUARTET NO. 5 (1995)   20'

A 6 LETTER LETTER (1996)   3'
for solo English horn

QUINTET (1997)   10'
for piano and string quartet

LUIMEN (1997)   12'
for trumpet, trombone, mandolin, guitar, harp,
and vibraphone

SHARD (1997)   3'
for solo guitar

TEMPO E TEMPI (1998)   15'
for soprano, violin, English horn, and bass clarinet

FRAGMENT NO. 2 (1999)   3'
for string quartet

TWO DIVERSIONS (1999)   8'
for solo piano

RETROUVAILLES (2000)   3'
for solo piano

4 LAUDS (1984-2000)   11'
for solo violin
   Statement – Remembering Aaron (1999)   3'
   Riconoscenza per Goffredo Petrassi (1984)   4'
   Rhapsodic Musings (2000)   2'
   Fantasy – Remembering Roger (1999)   3'

OBOE QUARTET (2001)   17'
for oboe, violin, viola, and cello

HIYOKU (2001)   4'
for two clarinets

STEEP STEPS (2001)   3'
for bass clarinet

AU QUAI (2002)   3'
for bassoon and viola

RETRACING (2002)   3'
for solo bassoon

CALL (2003)   1'
for two trumpets and horn

INTERMITTENCES (2005)   6'
for solo piano

HENDON MUSIC

BOOSEY & HAWKES

DISTRIBUTED BY

HAL•LEONARD®
CORPORATION
7777 W. BLUEMOUND RD. P.O. BOX 13819 MILWAUKEE, WI 53213

U.S. $10.95

8 84088 05461 8

HL48019134

ISBN-13: 978-1-4234-1033-1
Distributed By
HAL LEONARD
48019134   9 781423 410331

ISMN M-051-10445-1

for Oliver Knussen on his 50th birthday
with the greatest admiration and love

AU QUAI

Elliott Carter
(2002)

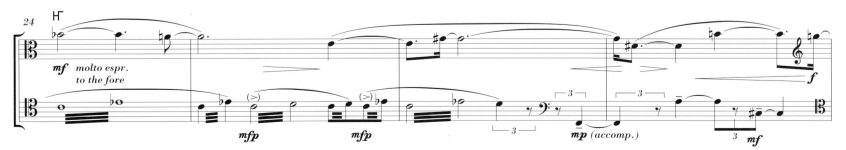

M-051-10445-1

Printed in U.S.A.

ELLIOTT CARTER

AU QUAI

for bassoon and viola

HENDON MUSIC

BOOSEY&HAWKES

DISTRIBUTED BY

HAL•LEONARD®